A NEW WORLD
Unconditional Love for Humanity
By Jerry Alatalo

I0440006

There are two ways that you can live your life: you can live as if nothing is a miracle; you can live as if everything is a miracle. -- Albert Einstein

Contents.

A. Higher Ground.

The seeker who sets out upon the way shines bright over the world.
–Sayings of the Buddha

We are going to attempt to create A New World. A Heaven on Earth.

Thank you for reading these words. We hope and pray that by your being here that everyone, everywhere on Earth will be helped and benefitted.

Let us imagine that we are sitting in the living room and having a pleasant conversation. We are simply human beings talking about all of the things that we as humans deal with. Hopefully our conversation will be of the type that is memorable. That type of conversation which is impossible to forget because there was a real and genuine understanding created that is felt viscerally because it is profound. One of those sharing of ideas that makes those who share the ideas glad that they did.

This is the goal of most writers. To articulate ideas in such a way that understanding is created and increased. As a result of this understanding folks are more at ease with each other. Writers and all artists attempt to communicate in a good way that increases the grand total in the tally of human agreements. A goal of writers and creative artists is to contribute in some concrete way to the elimination of misunderstanding and the increase of peace.

As public speaking is second to death on the list of things people fear most, writers/artists have to overcome all that is associated with the fear of public speaking. For someone to put their ideas and thoughts in the public arena, one risks criticism, attack, misunderstanding and disagreement. If the writer can be as honest as humanly possible then perhaps this risk may be minimized. For what it is worth know that this writer will be as honest as possible.

As someone who is relatively new to writing let us say that there is a lot of hopeful anticipation when starting a new project. One imagines that the completed work is successful. For different writers and artists there are a number of definitions of the word success regarding the finished work. This variance in perspectives regarding artistic success goes into the whole set of reasons that the creative artist makes the effort to produce the work in the first place.

And so it is useful to look at the various reasons creative people create. What do most people think when the word success is mentioned? It is safe to say that most people associate money with success. The more money that a person makes the more successful that person is perceived. This is the most popular definition of success. So in the mind of most people the more money you make the more successful you are. If you do not make a great deal of money then you are at risk of being perceived of as a failure.

Let us dig a little deeper into what is success and failure. It is very interesting to observe how differently people will behave when in the presence of a multi-millionaire as opposed to someone who is penniless. Is there anything in reality that actually separates the worth of one human being and another human being? When the multi-millionaire and the penniless person pass on to the spirit world will the Creator perceive their souls any differently?

For some creative artists the financial success of their work is their first and only definition of success. These artists have one goal for their completed work and that is to make as much money as they possibly can. For others it is a combination of factors that define success. These artists have more than one goal for their finished work. They have the goals of creating a work that makes a good difference in the lives of the people in the audience and makes them money. For other artists the only goal is to make a good difference in the lives of the people in the audience and the monetary aspect has no relevance whatsoever to their work.

This breakdown of the motivations and the definitions of success by artists illustrate the range of artistic efforts. This breakdown of motivations and definitions of success could correspond not only to artists but to everyone. Now there are various shades of thought between these three philosophies. One could see where there are people who are one hundred percent about making money, those who are ninety percent about making money and ten percent about making a good difference for the audience, those who are 75/25, 50/50, 25/75, 10/90 and zero percent about money or one hundred percent about making a good difference.

For this writer a lasting impression was made years ago after reading the book "What is Art?" by Russian writer Leo Tolstoy. Tolstoy is famous for his novels; most have heard of either "War and Peace" or "Anna Karenina". "What is Art" was a non-fiction book by Tolstoy where he attempted to determine what real art was and how it could be identified. Tolstoy was a writer of the highest integrity and honesty. We would recommend that you read "What is Art?" by Leo Tolstoy, especially if you are a creative artist.

We were in the university library looking for good books to read and came across a copy of Mohandes Gandhi's book "All Men Are Brothers", checked the book out of the library and read it. This is another good book suggestion, by the way. In Gandhi's book he mentioned Tolstoy's "What is Art?" and said he thought it was

Tolstoy's masterpiece. Of course after finishing Gandhi's book we had to read Tolstoy's. We had not read any Tolstoy books at that point as we were unaware of Tolstoy's non-fiction writing. We were aware that he was considered one of the all-time greatest novelists.

Luckily the same university library had a copy of Tolstoy's "What is Art?" and we were able to read it. As Gandhi mentioned that "What is Art?" was in his estimation Tolstoy's masterpiece. We were impressed with the book very much. The book was impressive for Tolstoy had a sense of quickly getting to the profound points. Probably because of his experiences in war Tolstoy was fully aware of his and our mortality. For this reason he would not allow himself to go halfway as a writer and an artist.

The words that Tolstoy wrote that were most memorable concerned his appraisal of the world of art in his time. Tolstoy believed that in order for a work to be considered art that the work had to be a vehicle for the transfer of the highest spiritual thought and feeling on the Earth. As a consequence of the artist making the effort to create the work and the audience experiencing the work, there is the actual transfer of the highest spiritual feeling on Earth.

The second criteria relates to the conveyance of the highest spiritual feeling on the Earth, in that the second major criteria for Tolstoy was that the work must result in a literal improvement in the conditions of life on the planet. After coming across the criterion Tolstoy developed for a creative work to be considered art we agree with his assessments. Tolstoy describes his experiences upon taking in plays (no television in Tolstoy's days) where he finds the work to be so shallow and disappointing that he must leave after the second act.

It was interesting after reading the book to think about Tolstoy's criterion when we viewed movies. We are all appreciative of those movies that move us to the point where we are stunned when we are walking out of the theater. We sit in our seat as the audience leaves the theater in order totally soak in the profound messages that the creators of the movie have just presented us with. We have to drink in every last drop of the movie. These are the artistic works which have an effect on the audience such that there is no doubt in the minds of those in the audience that this work is important.

These are the works that you have to recommend and suggest to others to experience. The same goes for any artistic work that takes the audience to that place of wonder, feeling and emotion where he or she is moved and literally changed. The work made a difference to the audience and most of the time the difference is positive. This means the criteria of literal improvement in the human condition described by Tolstoy.

So we begin to think about combining the criteria of literally improving the human condition and the transfer of the highest spiritual thought and feeling on Earth. The work that literally improves the human condition is good and is art because it met one of Tolstoy's criteria. On those rare occasions where the creative artist produces a work that both literally improves the human condition and also transfers the highest spiritual thought and feeling on Earth to the audience then one will see a masterpiece.

We suppose that every creative artist is in search of their masterpiece. All hope that after finishing the present work that they will be satisfied that they could not have done anything more, exerted more physical, mental or spiritual effort to reach their goals for the work. Their efforts were like those of athletes who describe after the contest that they "left it all on the field".

There are various reasons that artists have for creating.

We hold close the standards and tests of true art described by Leo Tolstoy. If this work does not result in the conveyance of the highest spiritual feeling on Earth at this time as well as literally improve the human condition then we will have failed to reach our goals.

Writing is a creative endeavor and it is very interesting to type your words to see where the project goes. We would recommend writing for everyone as one may come across an insight here or there that is changing and evolutionary. What we mean here by changing is the conscious awareness of evolution.

As we live our lives we are sometimes unconscious of change. The thing that is neat about writing and all creative artistic efforts is that the writer/artist finds a conscious awareness of growth and evolving. One could say that every form of creative effort gives the creative person this same awareness.

There are certain amounts of unwillingness or reticence to change and evolve. Some have a set, routine way of living and there is nothing that is going to change that routine. That is just the way it is. The statement "that is how it has always been" signifies a way of thinking that minimizes the potential for change and evolution of many types occurring at many levels.

"That is just the way it is." That statement points to a way of thinking that suggests that there is nothing that can be done to improve certain situations or conditions. This way of thinking many times shuts the door on the sharing of ideas which are centered on improving situations and conditions at all levels of human activity.

There is always room for improvement on this Earth. To rise to a more desirable or excellent condition or quality is the definition of to improve. The act of centering our thoughts on ways that life on Earth can be improved or raised to a more desirable or excellent condition is an artistic act. All those who think about ways to make the world a better place are artists if one understands Leo Tolstoy's definition of art.

All those who are spiritual seekers are artists. Those who are spiritual seekers are perpetually perceiving the highest feeling and thought on the planet. Whatever the current state of a spiritual seeker, it is the highest spiritual state that they have attained thus far in their life. As spiritual knowledge, wisdom and awareness increases through continual searching, that perpetual highest spiritual state correspondingly raises higher and higher.

How high can the human being's spiritual state rise? This is an extremely interesting question. There are those human beings who have read all of the great spiritual texts and thousands of books devoted to philosophy and spirituality. These men and women would seem to have exhausted every avenue in their searches for truth. They have attained a tremendous amount of knowledge, wisdom and insight.

The collective efforts of men and women through the ages to articulate on the great questions of humanity have been tremendous. Think of all of the books you have read. Think of all the conversations you have had with others on the big questions of life. As individuals our experiences amount to a considerable degree of thought and effort in the area of philosophy, spirituality and finding answers to the large questions about our existence.

Can we imagine the totality of human thought that has been devoted to the philosophical and spiritual questions that we all face?

We come to a point where we observe that of the billions and billions of thoughts the human race has had since the beginning of time there must be some absolute truth available. How does one identify absolute truth when one comes upon it? Does our search for absolute truth ever come to a successful conclusion? Absolute is defined as free from imperfection, complete, perfect and pure.

This beginning chapter is titled 'higher ground' as this work is the next stage of the climbing of the mountain. We are travelling upward in the search for absolute truth.

B. Helping Hands.

The one who has conquered himself is a far greater hero than he who has defeated a thousand times a thousand men. –Sayings of the Buddha

There is a way of thinking that proposes that the reason for living is to be of service to, and help, our fellow man. As we are writing these words there has been a weather disaster in the eastern region of the United States of America. Hurricane Sandy has been described as the most damaging storm ever to make landfall in this area around the states of New York and New Jersey. One has to start asking questions such as "Why would the Creator allow something so horrible to happen to people?"

Many lives were lost, many lost their homes and possessions, many billions of dollars of damages have occurred while many people have had to endure intense suffering. We are left speechless and numb after witnessing images of such a powerful cataclysm. Those who are not directly experiencing the cataclysm have empathy and compassion for those who are in the thick of the damages. Those who are able to help in any way have pitched in to help in the recovery.

We can say that the only bright side to these types of events is that humanity shows what it is capable of with regard to serving and helping our fellow man. Those who take the time, effort and initiative to reduce the suffering of their fellow men, women and children should be thanked for their heroic acts. The empathy and compassion that is expressed at times like these gives good evidence of an inner, built in quality of the human being.

An appreciation of this inner quality of humans is very important to consider. When circumstances and situations are such that action is required human beings take the steps which point to the highest spiritual feeling on Earth. Under such circumstances human beings take the actions that result in a literal improvement in the conditions of their fellow man.

We witness heroism on a grand scale. One witnesses folks who pitch in without even giving their efforts a second thought. Many do not stop to consider why they are helping as it just seems like the right thing to do. The phenomena of humans instinctually coming to the aid of their fellow humans in times of suffering is important to study and understand.

How can we explain the instinct of humans to help their fellow man in time of need? Perhaps the explanation of this human instinct is simply that this instinct is proof positive of the existence of unconditional Love in every single one of us.

One envisions the day when the reporter alters the wording of his or her report from "many have joined the recovery effort" to "many have given their unconditional Love to the recovery effort." Do you find it interesting that the words Love, unconditional Love or Infinite Love are rarely used and that there is a reticence or reluctance to say the words out loud? One has to think deeply to find an explanation for this reticence and reluctance.

Think of all the billions of words that are spoken by human beings all day, every day across this Earth. Next think about the percentage of those billions of words spoken daily that are or pertain to Love, unconditional Love or Infinite Love. We remember watching the actor Mickey Rooney on the Tonight Show with Johnny Carson many years ago. Mickey Rooney may have been in his mid to late 70's at that time. Mr. Rooney mentioned the word Love a few times and it felt while viewing this conversation that there was a line crossed by Mr. Rooney with the simple speaking of the word Love.

It was an odd feeling to watch this as it seemed that there was a palpable energy to move away from any discussion of Love. At the time we were interested in Mickey Rooney elaborating more on his Love experiences but it seemed that reticence and reluctance won the day. We know this seems like an insignificant story but we are trying to make a point.

Regarding the spiritual search for absolute truth many have come to the point where Love is the paramount factor found during that search. For humans to be reticent and reluctant to even speak the word Love seems to be a type of rejection of the utter importance of Love in the world. To illustrate our point let us imagine people being reticent and reticent to talk about water. Water is required by every living thing to continue living. There is no reluctance to speak the word water as all acknowledge the utter importance of water to physical survival.

Now we must answer the question: "Where is Love on the list of things that are utterly important to humans?" We would submit that Love is the most important power and substance in the universe.

One of the goals that the writer has for this work is placement of Love at the top of the list of the most important human concerns. For this assertion we run the risk of being labeled an idealist, optimist, perfectionist, reformer, visionary or one who belongs to the church of utopianism. So be it. We do not apologize for speaking of the utter importance of Love in this world.

Our idealist vision is a world that is fueled by Love where every decision made by human beings is based on Love. Call us an idealist. Call us a visionary. Call us anything. This new world is within the realm of possibility; it is achievable.

What is fueling this world now? As, whether human beings are aware of it or not, unconditional Love is built in to all of us there are varying manifestations of this unconditional Love happening all the time. One could say that the opposite of Love is fear. There are varying manifestations of fear happening all the time. Some believe that there are only two emotions in reality and that we as humans are coming from one, and only one, of these two emotions at all times. Those emotions are Love and fear. We are either operating from Love or fear at all times and we can always, at all times choose.

What we are suggesting is that every man, woman and child on this Earth can choose Love in every moment. How would we describe a world where every man, woman and child has chosen to come from the emotion of Love at each and every moment. For certain this could be described as A New World. It would be safe to say that humanity has created a Heaven on Earth.

We are painting a picture of a possible New World; a Heaven on Earth. The creation of this type of world is worth striving for. There is nothing to lose and everything to gain when humanity dares this effort. In our grandest vision this work can be seen as one of the matches that lights the fires of Love which will engulf and consume the entire world.

So accuse this writer of having delusions of grandeur. It does not matter as the evolution of the human race is going in this direction. Why should one settle for small dreams and goals? The creation of a New World, a Heaven on Earth, is the ultimate evolutionary destination that mankind could ever strive for. This striving results in no loss. This striving results in only gains for the human race and all of the creation.

Let us use a very simple analogy here. Imagine that you are going to drive your car to a certain destination. Now you realize that your car is out of gas. Once you put the gas in your tank you start your car, get on the road and drive to your destination. You arrive at your destination.

The gas that is required for the human race to arrive at the destination A New World/Heaven on Earth is unconditional Love.

It is interesting to observe how through the ages there have been men and women who have attempted to convey messages of Love for your fellow man and service to your human family in order to make the world a better place. What is both interesting and puzzling are those instances where men and women who conveyed such messages were somehow seen as threatening to others and ended up being the victims of assassinations.

Jesus Christ is the most well known of those who were assassinated for bringing the message of Love for your fellow man. Muhammad had attempts on his life. Mohandes Gandhi was shot and killed. Martin Luther King was assassinated. Many men and women who were never as famous as these have been killed in the name of Love through the ages. For one to try to understand the phenomena is a great challenge.

Let us try to think deeply about this. What in the world is happening when humans kill another because that other is attempting to make the world a better place and reduce suffering? It would seem that one factor here is the love of money. Another factor that seems to part of the equation is power and control of others. Another would be ego and the belief in separation and superiority. These seem to be major factors where change in the form of the creation of a better, new world is fought ferociously.

Those who tried to create a better world stressed the equality of human beings so this threatened those who were unequal in terms of money and material things. Christ, Muhammad, Gandhi and King proposed serving your fellow man so this threatened those who had a lust for power and control as well as those who believed that they were separate and superior to others. The awareness that Christ, Muhammad, Gandhi and King as well as many other men and women peacemakers were seen as threats by others is astonishing.

It would seem that the time has arrived where the obliteration of the type of thinking that sees those who are trying to create a better world as threatening is required. Perhaps folks simply will live lives of unconditional Love and the power of example will be unstoppable. Forgiveness is a very important concept to understand. One could see that all of the hurtful actions that humans take are cries for Love.

Forgiveness was best exemplified by Jesus when on the cross he said "Forgive them Father. They know not what they do." Forgiveness is an action that requires some thought to understand. Can one imagine the tremendous Love that Jesus showed when he forgave those who took his life? This has to be the highest Love in the universe; comprehension of the immensity of that Love is an effort which must, when taken, lead to absolute truth.

Think about those situations where a misunderstanding has separated family members for many years. Perhaps someone said words that were hurtful, something petty or insignificant and instead of forgiving, the person who the words were directed at held a grudge. If Jesus could forgive those who took his life how ridiculous we must look for not being able to forgive someone for a petty, stupid remark.

Tell that person that you forgive them with your words if possible. Understand that nobody in their right mind would do anything to hurt another. The person who hurts another in any way is crying out for Love. Understand that when you hurt another in any way that you are crying out for Love. Apologize to the other and communicate sincerely so that you may be friends. Then do not forget to forgive yourself.

What kind of a difference are we making? When we follow our highest thoughts of Love and forgiveness we eliminate stress and the difference is that we are more joyful and healthy. Holding on to negative emotions like anger, resentment and revenge contribute to our disease and results in unhealthy minds, bodies, spirits and relationships. Let go of all negative thoughts and emotions. They are not good for you or others. Embrace Love and forgiveness and you can look forward to more health, joy and peace.

Trust your conscience and you will be the better for it. With regard to negative thoughts you can eliminate them. It may seem difficult at first but it will become easier and easier if you try. We remember the words of a Native American healer when he said "If there was one piece of advice I could give to others it is to never complete a negative thought." You can eliminate negative thoughts. It is well worth any effort that you take.

Just as an individual can eliminate negative thoughts so can the world. When more and more human beings hold to the goal of creating a better world then negative thoughts will occur less and less until all people have a healthy, optimistic outlook for the future. The human race can eliminate negative thoughts. It is well worth any effort that humanity takes.

Once the human race comprehends the absolute potential of creating a better world and then accepts the challenge to create A New World, then there is nothing that can stop the reaching of that goal. We hope and pray that humanity makes good decisions and takes the steps necessary to create a world that all will be proud to pass on to the generations that come. We thank the Creator that we could perhaps contribute in any way to help in the creation of a new and better world.

C. Love of Money.

In order to swim one takes off all one's clothes—in order to aspire to the truth one must undress in a far more inward sense, divest oneself of all one's inward clothes, of thoughts, conceptions, selfishness, etc., before one is sufficiently naked. –Soren Kierkegaard

Here we will try to identify the most important issues facing humanity now which, depending on how humans handle them, will directly affect future generations. The observations that are made will require humility in order to avoid any form of judgment. As all are responsible for their decisions and actions it is not for this writer to judge anyone. We will simply make observations on what is occurring on Earth and offer our thoughts for consideration.

The examination of current Earth realities is a challenge in that the issues of importance involve very powerful entities and institutions. We have gone into this area in previous writings but need to review for those who are not aware of such writings. Perhaps we will be more concise and come at this in a way that results in greater understanding and agreement. To be honest with you we do not enjoy delving into these issues.

Looking at these issues is not an activity that is looked forward to. We would wish that some of the activities we are about to describe were not existent. As they exist we have no alternative but to expose them with the hope that humanity will think of future generations and act for the good of those future generations. We will cover issues of major concern first and descend in order of importance.

1. Genetic modification of food, animals and other life forms.

As all living things on Earth require food to survive we believe that the greatest concern for the human race at this time is the genetic modification of food, crops, animals and other life forms. The science that has been developed to create patentable life forms such as corn, soybeans, wheat, cotton, canola and more frankly scares one to death. When one considers the negative consequences that go along with the planting and harvesting of these crops one is left with a combination of extremely strong emotions, the strongest being compassion and anger.

First what gives people the right to interfere with the natural world in such a way as to threaten nature and its beauty and bounty? What kind of leaders would allow untested biological technology to be inserted into the natural world? Genetically modified organisms (GMO'S) are the greatest threat to life on planet Earth that humanity has ever seen.

Let us begin with describing a horrific scientific creation that is called the terminator seed. This is a genetically modified seed that commits suicide after one planting. Excuse me folks but does this not strike you as totally insane? The reason that Monsanto created terminator seeds is to sell more seeds. Farmers have since the beginning of time, in their farming practices, saved seeds for the next season's planting. As these seeds kill themselves there is nothing for the farmers to save. The farmers have to buy the seeds form a business entity at next season's planting time.

For a government to approve the use of such a product is nothing short of criminal. It is no stretch of the imagination to say that these seeds will be carried in one way or another into the surrounding lands, plant life and animal life. In a very real sense this type of product can be compared to a cancer let loose on the environment. One shudders to think of the possible negative consequences that will occur because of the placement of this cancerous technology. We strongly advocate for the complete abolishment of genetically modified foods. For the sake of humanity and its continuance as a species, please ban this threat.

Can we imagine the problems associated with the spread of this horrid life form? Think about what will be the result of cross pollination when the wind, birds, animals, man or insects move this plant equivalent of radioactive waste around the environment. The human race must become aware of this threat as soon as possible so that it can be stamped out now. There is absolutely no time to waste in the elimination of this monstrous error.

That this issue is rarely if ever discussed in the mainstream media is an important observation. What we see here is a form of censorship in media corporations. There are a number of possible explanations for the censoring of certain issues by the major media. First would be the fact that major media companies depend on advertisers for their income and any story that they report on which would cause a company to stop advertising with them is not going to air. Second there are many men and women on the boards of directors at many corporations.

You have people sitting on numerous boards of directors so if the media company airs a report which shows one corporation in a negative light not only does that corporation stop running ads but all the rest stop as well. This is the reason that you will rarely see a negative story about corporate actions that shine a negative light on that corporation. A large percentage of the population gets their information from the mainstream media. This is the reason that many people are uninformed or misinformed about the realities on Earth.

As alternative media, especially on the internet, has grown tremendously humanity has been catching up with the realities on the planet that have been unreported on the major media outlets for many years. People have been taking matters into their own hands with regard to getting the truth to their fellow men and women on issues of importance such as GMO food. One can easily go on the internet and watch the excellent documentaries "The World According To Monsanto" and "Food, Inc.".

If you have not watched these documentaries please do so as they are important messages for humanity. A number of countries have learned the dangers of GMO food and crops and have written laws requiring the labeling of GMO foods, while some have gone so far as banning GMO food or crops from their lands. We would suggest strongly, as already mentioned but worth mentioning again, that GMO food and crops be banished from the face of the Earth.

If you have not yet been convinced that you need to inform yourself, your family and friends on the dangers of GMO foods and crops the following information will get your energy moving to do something to stop this insane technology. Cotton farmers in the country of India have seen GMO cotton introduced into their country a number of years ago. The corporate owners of the patents on cotton promised increased yields and less costs on inputs such as chemical fertilizers and pesticides.

What occurred was the exact opposite of the corporate promises. Yields ended up being lower, chemical input costs went up and farmers now were at the mercy of seed companies as terminator seeds cannot be saved for next season's planting. Many cotton farmers in India ran into financial problems and lost their farms. What we are about to share with you is very tough to hear but you must know. Estimates are that 250,000 farmers in India have committed suicide in the last fifteen years. This is a scandal of worldwide proportions and no major media company has reported it with the investigation required for such a monumental reality.

We must be honest with you when we say to you that we have a very difficult time dealing with the reality of this condition on the planet. For the love of money and profits a group of people have created these products and have not realized the error of their actions and ceased. For a third time we must say that GMO foods and crops must be banned from the Earth now.

You can find personal accounts from farmers who have been treated unfairly, and frankly despicably, by GMO corporations (namely Monsanto) on the internet. The story of Mr. Percy Schmeiser, a canola farmer from Canada will be all you need to learn about to get your blood boiling. Find videos on Youtube by typing Percy Schmeiser Monsanto in the search box. If after watching the story of Percy Schmeiser and his terrible treatment by Monsanto you do not feel a need to act then there is no justice in this world.

Mr. Schmeiser is a fine man and a hero in our mind. The world's people must learn what is happening to a large number of fine people who are farmers and have run into the Monsanto evil machine. We have no apology to offer when using the term evil in the same sentence as Monsanto. Our appraisal is that this corporation defines the word evil. We understand that there are those who are employed by Monsanto who are decent folks who need to earn a living.

We would think that a corporation like Monsanto would reconsider the direction they have taken and decide to go in that direction which helps farmers be successful at growing good food for people. GMO food is not as nutritious or as good tasting as God given foods without any manipulation. Farms which are planted with GMO seed have lower yields than organic, straight food farms. On every level GMO foods and crops lose and lose in the biggest and worst way.

The human race and all life on this planet loses as long as this scourge continues to exist.

Scientists who have discovered the harmful effects of GMO food consumption have been fired and blacklisted. Folks, this is an issue which the whole world must become fully informed about very, very soon. Please consider doing whatever you can to get informed about this issue and then take powerful preventive action as soon as possible.

Today is November 7, 2012 and yesterday saw Barack Obama re-elected President of the United States of America. Yesterday California voters defeated a ballot initiative calling for the labeling of foods which contained GMO's. The measure was defeated by a 58 to 42 vote. Monsanto, DuPont and other corporations involved in the genetic food and animal modification business spent an estimated 50 million dollars on advertising to defeat the measure.

These GMO corporations know for a fact that the labeling of GMO foods is the beginning of the end. Thankfully the people of the Earth will rise up to defeat this GMO monster.

We pray that those in positions of power at the corporations involved with the genetic modification of foods, crops, animals and other life forms will come to understand the harm that is being inflicted. We ask them humbly to change course now and we offer forgiveness.

2. Monetary reform.

Next we will delve into the disturbing world of financial systems. We would say that the negative consequences of private monetary systems for humanity that have occurred for hundreds of years ranks a close second on the list of the most important concerns for the human race. As every living person, animal and plant needs food for survival, the elimination of genetically modified foods, crops, animals and other life forms is the number one urgent concern for mankind.

The issue of monetary reform could begin with a definition of the word usury. Usury is defined as the practice of lending money and charging the borrower interest, especially at an exorbitant and illegal rate. Perhaps recently many of you have become aware of the so-called LIBOR scandal (London inter-bank offered rate) which has been called "The Wall Street scandal" and the "scandal of all scandals". Banks from around the world participate in setting the LIBOR interest rate and it has come to light that interest rate fixing has taken place.

This means that all people who take on loans for housing, automobiles, credit cards, or any loans of whatever type or reason, have been gouged on interest payments for God only knows how many years. Many have lost their homes because of these rigged high interest rates. This scandal is a shocking indictment of the banks and makes Bernie Madoff look like a boy scout. Many trillions of dollars have been siphoned off of customers through loans and credit cards as a result of the conspiracy between major banks to manipulate interest rates.

So Barclays bank pays $455 million in fines for their actions in this scandal. Can regulators determine how many billions or trillions that they netted? If any one of us ripped off one of our neighbors for $10,000 would our punishment be a $1,000 fine? When one delves into the workings of the financial sector and finds scandal after scandal one comes to a point where they experience scandal fatigue.

In terms of financial power we are going up against the largest financial powers on Earth. Through the generations of history there have been a group of families that have consolidated financial power to an extent that is hard to fathom. Since the time when banking began there have been a handful of people who have come to dominate the banking industry and have fought against any regulations by governments to slow down their desire for more and more profits.

God bless the fine men and women who work in the financial sector of the economy in order to provide for their families. These are good people who are doing what they can to put food on the table and clothes on their children. We do not wish to have anyone place any type of blame at the feet of these.

Where the problem rests with regard to scandal, corruption, deception and greed is at the feet of the "big dogs". Those who have used their financial power to kill regulations and pave the way for fraudulent financial acts to be committed with impunity are the actors to deal with. These people are the money junkies. As opposed to sound, honest bankers who run their banks in a decent way by loaning at fair interest, where those who work at the bank can be paid and investors make a modest return, the unfortunate situation at too many banks is that the mad race to increase profits in the biggest way has become the norm of operations.

Please keep in mind during this discussion of monetary reform that Jesus forgave those that killed him. At risk of being labeled the greatest conspiracy theorist of all time we remember that the only description of a time where Jesus showed anger was when he confronted the moneychangers. He overturned the tables of the moneychangers. This was because they were exploiting the poor.

And he taught, and said to them, "Is it not written, 'my house shall be called a house of prayer for all nations'? But you have made it a den of robbers." And the chief priests and the scribes heard it and sought a way to destroy him; for they feared him, because the multitude was astonished at his teaching. Mark 11: 17-18

Is it possible that Jesus was killed because he tried to protect the poor from exploitation?

As mentioned previously it is hard to figure out why those who have the largest impact on creating a more Loving, just and peaceful world come to a place where others seek to destroy them.

The scenario with Jesus and the moneychangers has a direct relation to the commandment "You shall Love your neighbor as yourself." When Jesus saw the evidence of the moneychangers exploiting the poor he reacted with righteous anger. This exploitation of the poor was seen by Jesus as a direct contradiction of the commandment.

What has been occurring in the present days of the world of money and finance is no different then what occurred on the day that Jesus walked into the temple and overturned the tables of the moneychangers.

God bless those men and women of integrity and honesty who have told the truth of what is really happening in the financial sector. These men and women are to be greatly thanked for relaying the experiences they had while working and operating inside of the system. Given the damage done to the lives of billions of people on

Earth by the reckless gambling of those in the major financial centers of New York and London, those who are speaking truth to power are overturning the tables of today's moneychangers,

Thankfully the truth of what has been occurring in the world regarding monetary systems and the financial sector is now easy for anyone to find on the internet. Find the story of Brooksley Born on PBS' Frontline edition titled "The Warning" to cut to the chase and become informed about the 1,500 trillion dollar derivatives market. If your present stance on regulation of the financial sectors around the world is one of less regulations, then this Frontline story will change your mind in a New York minute. You will be calling for tremendously effective regulations and enforcement while demanding real prison time for those who commit financial fraud.

 Find the book "Bailout" by Neil Barofsky, the former Inspector General for the government's TARP program. Barofsky points out how the TARP funds were used in a way that benefitted the too big to fail corporations on Wall Street at the expense of main street and struggling homeowners.

Find the book "Bull By The Horns" by Sheila Bair who was head of the FDIC (Federal Deposit Insurance Corporation) during the years 2006-2011. In 2008 and 2009 Forbes magazine named her the second most powerful woman in the world. Her frank account of what happened in the turbulent years 2007-2008 will help you to gain an immense knowledge of the workings of the financial system in America.

Find and watch the Academy award winning documentary "Inside Job" by Charles Ferguson. Ferguson and his documentary offer a real analysis of what happened that led to the economic crises of 2008. This documentary is must see for anyone who is interested in learning the truth of what happened on Wall Street which resulted in the worst economic downturn since the great depression. Charles Ferguson went to the podium to accept his Oscar for best documentary and said to the billion people watching the Academy Awards, "Two years after the financial crisis and not one financial executive has gone to jail. That is wrong."

Find Charles Ferguson's book "Predator Nation" which he published a few years after making "Inside Job" and you will find the most direct description of what has occurred in the banking and financial services industry. If you do not want to waste any time finding the real facts behind the economic crisis being felt on a world-wide scale go straight to "Inside Job" and then to "Predator Nation. Simply put Charles Ferguson is a hero and you will be overwhelmed by the messages of both his documentary and book.

What these men and women have to say is not for entertainment purposes. They are describing real events that have enormous consequences for the human race.

As we mentioned genetic modification of foods, crop, animals and other life forms is the number one issue of grave concern for humanity. The present day reality of monetary systems of the world, and negative economic consequences which are occurring on a planetary scale because of lack of needed reform, is a close second.

Find and watch the Bill Still documentary "The Secret of Oz". In the documentary Mr. Still gives the viewer a very well detailed history of money and offers the viewer great knowledge in the field of monetary systems. We recommend "The Secret of Oz" documentary for those of you who want to go straight to the facts about money and how the control of the supply of money has affected economies around the Earth.

Let us first make sure that a popular misconception is corrected. What do you think the Federal Reserve Sysytem is? Take a minute to ponder the question. Please take a minute to ponder the question as we are trying to correct a major misconception which has very large consequences in the real world. Probably many of you have thought about what the Federal Reserve is and your conclusion is that it is the branch of the United States government in charge of printing money.

We would guess that a high percentage of those who are reading these words have the same image of the Federal Reserve. A public institution that is along the lines of the Department of the Interior, the Department of Education, the Justice Department etc..

The Federal Reserve Act of 1913 established the Federal Reserve System and regional banks with central banking authority for the United States of America for a period of 100 years.

The Federal Reserve is a private bank owned by private shareholders.

We will repeat the last sentence so that there is no doubt that the popular misconception is corrected.

The Federal Reserve is a private bank owned by private shareholders.

After you watch the Frontline program "The Warning" about Brooksley Born, after you have read "Bailout" by Neil Barofsky, after you have read "Bull by the Horns" by Sheila Bair, after you have watched the documentary "Inside Job" by Charles Ferguson, after reading Charles Ferguson's book "Predator Nation" and watched Bill Still's documentary "The Secret of Oz" you will have enough knowledge to come to the conclusion that the Federal Reserve 100 year charter should not be renewed in 2013.

If you are not big on books then watch first "The Secret of Oz", second "Inside Job" and then the Brooksley Born Frontline program.

These three programs alone will give you a very good foundation of knowledge to appreciate the need to take the control of the money supply away from private corporations and place that control in the Federal government. In other words "End the Fed".

Let us imagine some similar scenarios to private banks in control of a country's money supply. Can you imagine the federal government granting a 100 year charter to corporations, whose sole business was selling water, to control the entire nation's water supply? Would you want to see big oil corporations given a 100 year charter to control the entire nation's energy supply? How about giving the corporate food cartel a 100 year charter to control the food supply of the entire nation?

Imagine all the insider trading, sweet deals, manipulation of markets, corruption and fraud that have occurred since 1913. Do you think that those who are super-rich have not had enough time to devise ways to manipulate economic conditions for their own profit? The Federal Reserve was audited for the first time in a top to bottom way in 2011 and discovered 16 trillion dollars was secretly used to bailout banks and corporations all around the globe in the form of loans at 0.01% interest. Would you be ok if your mortgage loan interest was 0.01%?

Let us simply say it. The game is rigged. We were in the suburbs of Chicago and noticed after the bailouts of too big to fail banks that there were Chase banks being built on every valuable corner of real estate everywhere. The concerns of the average middle class and poor in America are down on the list of for those who hold the power and influence. This is increased concentration of wealth happening right before our eyes.

The banks and financial services sector of the economy have been allowed to operate in a casino atmosphere where extremely large, risky bets are common, resulting in terrible consequences for the economies of the world. Large financial business entities own the federal government and set the rules for themselves. Thousands of corporate lobbyists descend on Washington every day with campaign contributions to buy both sides of any debate.

America has returned to the same conditions of the 1920's with regard to wealth and income inequality. Greed is the name of the game. We have come to the point where the top1% makes 23.5% of the total income, which is more than the bottom 50% of the people. The top 1% in the 1970's made 8% of the total income in America, in the 1980's this rose to 14%, in the 1990's this rose to 19% until today's figure of 23.5%. The top one-tenth of 1% earns 12% of the total income in America.

America has the most unequal distribution of wealth among its populace of any major country on Earth.

Let us catch our breath here for a moment. Folks, the people who are involved in the fraud, corruption and all the rest are people just like everyone else. We are torn between demanding that they be hung in the streets, to making examples of them by sending financial fraud criminals to "real" jails, to contributing to the awareness of the people where there is a citizen's movement that is unstoppable.

Perhaps the ideal outcome will come about where the control of America's money supply will be taken away from private corporations in the form of the Federal Reserve and taken over by the national government as a public service institution. This seems to be the best prescription to stop the booms and busts caused by central bank manipulations of the economy. Central bank control of the quantity of money in the economy is not just an American problem.

All one has to do is look at what is happening in the European Union. Greece, Spain, Portugal, Italy and Ireland are suffering with depressions and austerity measures which are threatening public insurrections. Perhaps the example of Iceland should be followed. The people of Iceland threw out banks who fraudulently strapped the country with debt. The people of Iceland simply decided that enough was enough.

Read "The Confessions of an Economic Hit Man" by John Perkins to learn the inside information of the world geopolitical strategies of the powerful. Perkins, in his role as an economic hit man, would visit with the leaders of countries whose natural resources were coveted by multi-national corporations. He would arrange large loans from the World Bank or International Monetary Fund for the country to build up infrastructure in order to facilitate the harvest of national resources. These natural resources could be oil or minerals or whatever valuable national resource had been identified by those who wanted them.

When the country invariably ran into difficulty repaying the World Bank or IMF loans, Perkins would come back to the leader and offer him and his family great wealth if he allowed the multi-national corporations access at a low price to his country's natural resources. A wealthy few in the country would gain more wealth while the majority of the people would suffer austerity measures so that the World Bank or IMF loans could be repaid.

If the leader did not go along with Perkins' suggestions then Perkins would point out that the leader of the neighboring country recently died in an airplane crash. If the threat of assassination did not work then there were attempts made to change leadership in the country by coup or instigating uprisings by the people. If that did not work then the jackals were sent in to try to assassinate the leader.

If assassination was not successful then a war is started. This is what happened in Iraq. This scenario has unfortunately been the pattern for far too long. Leaders of countries have been assassinated or replaced through coups. Wars have been started and fought over natural resources for hundreds of years.

The writing of this information never ceases to bring a sadness. The awareness of the historical record of man's inhumanity to his fellow man brings an amount of disappointment at such a level that one sometimes wishes that they had never learned of such things.

Sitting back and reflecting for a moment, the realization of the truth found in the biblical passage "The love of money is the root of all evil." has an overwhelming affect. When one comes to see that the love of money really is the root of all evil it causes a certain amount of distress, as then one must decide what to do about it. Perhaps sharing this information with others will help in some way to decrease the love of money in this world.

As more human beings come to the conclusion that greed is an undesirable quality and leads to loss, then perhaps steps will be taken to eliminate greed in this world. Good changes will come as a natural process when this awareness is gained by the people of the planet.

3. Global climate change.

Being born and raised in the North country on Lake Superior we have seen the changes in the weather through the years. When we were small kids we would have snow in great amounts and would figure out how to play in whatever blizzard conditions came. School was regularly cancelled because of snowstorms where many inches of snow would fall. We had snow on the ground from November to April.

Years later we would notice while driving from Chicago for Christmas that it was raining on Christmas and there was no snow on the ground. We have no memory from childhood where the ground was without snow at Christmas.

Then in 2012 we had many days in a row in the month of March where the temperature was above 80 degrees. All of these days set record highs for the temperature. So it seems that one does not need the proof from scientists to know that global climate change is real.

This does not mean that we do not greatly appreciate the work of those scientists who are concerned about the environmental effects of climate change. Those who live in a more temperate climate don't have the evidence in their face. The work and studies of climate scientists are of value to convince people of the reality that those in the north experience directly. Just as the previous issues are argued by different groups according to their stakes in the results of decisions regarding those issues, global climate change is no different.

Those who are involved in oil, coal or other industries that science has pointed to for causes of the climate changes, will flat out say that global warming is bunk. Oil, coal and other industries will produce their own scientific evidence that there is no such thing as global warming. The average citizen will not see a thorough investigation on their television sets as media corporations do not want to upset oil companies and risk losing advertising revenue.

The hurricane named Sandy that crashed into New Jersey and New York at the end of October 2012 is seen as a wakeup call for the human race to finally come to grips on the issue of global warming. The storm Sandy was the most violent storm ever in the New York and New Jersey area. There have been a great number of destructive environmental events in recent years that point to severe problems with the weather.

Warmest year on record was in 2012. Rising sea levels are a large part of the problem concerning global climate change. As oceans rise coastal cities and their people are in greater danger and threat of damage and suffering. The number of events like hurricane Sandy can be expected to increase in the years ahead as humanity gets its act together by first recognizing the reality of weather problems.

As mentioned you will not see any serious discussion of global climate change, monetary reform or genetically modified organisms on the mainstream media. It is time that those who own the media corporations come to their senses and deal with these issues in the serious way that is required. After years of disappointment from the major media it will come down to the people to take the world in its hands and make the necessary changes.

It seems that just as individuals sometimes have to learn the hard way, the same can be said for mankind. Do not get me wrong here. We are extremely optimistic because the human race is getting the true realities of what is happening on Earth. This is a good thing. People from all around the planet are communicating in a good way. The result of this good communication is that people all around the planet are being thoughtful and honest with each other about the conditions on Earth

Because of this increase in good, thoughtful and honest communication by men, women and children all over the globe, issues like GMO's, monetary reform and global climate change are being discussed in serious ways. So to heck with the media, humanity is taking matters into its own hands and not waiting for those who do not express concern for the welfare of their fellow brothers and sisters on the planet.

As sea ice has rapidly been melting recently the result is greatly accelerated warming of the oceans. There has been a decrease in the difference in temperatures at the poles and the equator. What happens because of this is that jet streams slow down and storms are longer lasting in the areas they move across. Another result is that there is more moisture in the atmosphere which means larger storms. Flooding has become more prevalent and storms are changing latitudes. Forests are stressed because of these changes so there are more forest die-offs.

With the increased melt rates of polar ice large storms break up the ice and accelerate the melting even more. Ice at the Arctic rose a foot recently due to rising levels, so warmer ocean water filled the volume that moved and this accelerated the ice melt. Folks, the ice at the poles is melting now at an incredible rate. All one has to do is open their eyes for evidence of climate change. That there are those who still deny climate change suggests that we are surely living in an Orwellian society.

The issue of climate change was proven years ago and now humanity suffers the consequences of inaction. There now will be an increase in discussions between peoples all over the world on this issue. There will be a consensus reached by people all around the Earth which will start an unstoppable movement to act. The images seen around the world from areas devastated by hurricane Sandy will cause many to stand up and take action. Sorry folks but we mentioned earlier that these issues are tough to write about as we have seen the evidence, and the lack of action, for long enough.

There are many actions that can be taken to slow down those negative human activities that contribute to global warming. Energy efficiency in homes, automobiles and appliances would be good for employment as well as save people money on energy bills. Retrofitting homes with solar panels would be a start in America; many homes in Europe have panels on their roofs. Perhaps it is time for America to get the ball rolling with renewable energy units for homes. How about a Manhattan project for alternative energy solutions?

The country of Brazil has an alcohol production capacity that fuels 90% of their cars. Two of the advantages of alcohol used to fuel vehicles are that alcohol is both half the cost of gasoline and less polluting. Gasoline is subject to breakdown, alcohol never breaks down. Alcohol fuel for cars can be produced on a small scale by mom and pop businesses anywhere which would be a boon for the economy and employment statistics in America and other countries. Any alcohol produced in America reduces the amount of oil that has to be imported from other countries.

Find David Blume on the internet. He has a website, www.alcoholcanbeagas.com, which contains very important information on the tremendous potential of alcohol production in America and around the world. The pluses of going in the direction of alcohol fuel, for cars as well as electricity generation, are such that it is almost criminal that everyone is not aware of this most viable option. Once again we have corporations like oil and coal that do not want anyone slicing into their pie.

As trees are important for taking in carbon dioxide the growing of industrial hemp would reduce the number of trees that are harvested for paper and lumber. Hemp was the first plant cultivated for fiber use. There are many products that can be made with hemp including textiles which are more breathable and ten times stronger than cotton, bio-diesel fuels, bricks, chipboard, foods with high protein content, oils with favorable omega fats content and plastics.

Industrial hemp is now grown in many countries around the world including France, China, England, Germany, Switzerland, Canada and others. Hemp grows very quickly and takes half the inputs of water and chemicals as cotton. The wait time for cultivation of industrial hemp is many years shorter than pulp. Industrial hemp grows anywhere so anyone can go into farming it and making money.. Once again there are corporations who do not want anyone slicing into their profits pie. With unemployment levels where they are, here is one more viable option that would strengthen the economy and employ people.

Industrial hemp has none of the active ingredients that cause the marijuana high. The reason industrial hemp is illegal in the United State of America is because powerful interests want no competition. How American is that? Did someone say the land of the free, free enterprise and rugged individualism?

It seems that we can come to the conclusion that powerful, vested corporate interests have a large say in the decisions made by lawmakers at both the state and federal government levels.

So we as society must settle for blocked solutions and threats to the lives and well being of ourselves, our children and grandchildren in order to assure continuing levels of profits for dominant corporations. Is this what Americans are going to settle for? This is the best that we have got?

There are great, positive changes on the horizon for mankind. We profoundly thank all men, women and children who think about ways to create a better world for this and future generations.

D. Vote for Love.

The thought manifests as the word; The word manifests as the deed; The deed develops into habit; and habit hardens into character; So watch the thought and its ways with care, and let it spring from Love born out of concern for all beings... As the shadow follows the body, as we think, so we become. –Sayings of the Buddha

Many of us have watched sporting events on television or in person where we saw one the referees throw someone out of the game. The player gets ejected because he was not being sportsmanlike by fighting, cursing or being disrespectful of other competitors, coaches or the officials.

We are using the metaphor of the official ejecting the player to compare it to what we are about to discuss. The game is political power and elections. The player we are going to eject is money.

Election reform seems to be long overdue in America. Should democracy be for sale? Democracy is a form of government in which all eligible citizens have an equal say in the decisions that affect their lives. Do you have an equal say in the decisions that affect you and your family? Do you have an equal say on genetically modified organisms, the monetary system and the privately run Federal Reserve System, global climate change or any of a number of other issues of great consequence for you and humanity?

By definition America is not a democracy because people simply do not have an equal say in the decisions that affect their lives. What average citizen is going to match the tremendous sums of money being spent on advertising by extremely wealthy individuals during this 2012 election season?

The Supreme Court decision in the Citizens United v. Federal Election Commission case was the most undemocratic action ever taken in this country. This decision by the Supreme Court allows corporations and wealthy individuals to spend unlimited amounts of money on elections. What this means is that whoever has the most money wins. The corporations and the wealthy cannot give unlimited amounts to candidates but can spend unlimited amounts on advertising or paying for events or any of a number of other expenditures.

Those who would argue for the Citizens United decision would say that corporations or billionaires cannot give money directly to candidates. Anyone watching the advertising this 2012 election cycle understand that the logic used by those who are pro-Citizens United is totally flawed

Advertising by billionaires is obviously supporting a candidate. Smoke and mirrors. End of story.

Score one for democracy, right? The only way to overturn this wrong decision is passage of a constitutional amendment. There are petitions on the internet that you can sign. You can write a letter to the editor or post on a blog site. Please help in any way that you can to get this amendment passed. Negate this tremendous blunder.

We have an idea what an actual democracy would look like. How about we start with taking every last red cent out of the political process? This would mean no more political advertisements of any type anywhere. Not on television, radio, the internet, newspapers, lawn signs, bumper stickers, mailings; not anywhere. Make it illegal to advertise for any election at any level of government. The era of those having the most money to "sell" their candidate needs to end.

We would not be surprised if you would be ok with never seeing another political advertisement. Imagine an election reform that results in candidates for office having only one way to earn votes. This would be by the selling of their ideas. How original. If you convince the voters that your ideas are stronger than your opponent, then they vote for you.

Perhaps there would be an allowance for corporations and the wealthy to pay for many lengthy debates between the candidates (and that means all candidates including so-called third parties) where there is a thorough examination and comparison of ideas. Surely the corporations and wealthy would be eager to contribute to the restoration of democracy in America, right?

The most positive effect of election reform which allows only the communication of ideas through debate and questioning is that both the candidates and the voters will have no distractions to interfere with their thinking. As elections are important, because decisions are made at all levels of governance which have a real affect on peoples' lives and well being, thinking about humanity's conditions without distraction leads to the making of good decisions.

The current situation regarding elections contains so many distractions that it is a wonder that any significant thinking on important matters occurs at all. As we are writing these words on November 7, 2012 the United States of America has just elected Barack Obama as President for a second four year term. During this election cycle what level of thought have you experienced concerning the most important issues on planet Earth?

Have there been any discussions of genetically modified organisms and the threats of such creations?

Have you seen any mention of the monetary system and possible options including the transfer of control of the quantity of money from private corporations in the form of the Federal Reserve to a public service institution inside the federal government and controlled by the people?

What was there learned about the reality of global climate change and all of the consequences for humanity and life on this Earth?

Given that the airwaves are owned by the people the amount of time devoted to lengthy debates on the important issues for humanity should be given freely by media corporations. During an election cycle it would not be difficult for every cable provider to devote one channel wholly to debates. Let us say that candidate A challenges candidates B, C and D to a debate on genetically modified organisms. If candidates B and D decline to debate on genetically modified organisms then candidates A and C will be given a half hour to an hour of free airtime on the election channel to express his or her thoughts to the voters.

There are a variety of possible formats that could be created where every candidate would be given ample time to share their ideas with voters. Perhaps the election channel will start airing candidate debates four months prior to the day of the election. Perhaps debates will begin three months prior to the day of the election.

What we are trying to envision and articulate to you is an election process where there is a much greater communication of ideas to the point where good decisions will be made and humanity stands to realize improvement and gain. There will be a much higher level of discussion created which can only result in an increase of more positive outcomes. Simply put the current election process has far too many distractions to allow the genuine sharing of ideas. Any distractions to the real and honest communications between candidates and voters should be eliminated.

Instituting this concept would create an election process that is fairer, more decent and result in movement toward a condition called true democracy. The election process will become transparent where nothing can be hidden or run away from. Issues of concern for humanity will be addressed head on and dealt with. Non-issues will be recognized as non-issues and the whole world of thought surrounding governance and decision making will be elevated to a much higher moral, ethical and, most importantly, spiritual level.

No longer will those who chose to try to serve their fellow man in the political arena spend any time on raising money or thinking about the construction of their advertising effort. If the person is disingenuous, insincere or calculating those who hear their ideas and compare those ideas to the other candidates will discern correctly who is sincere much more often. We must believe that every single voter wants to elect men and women to office who are sincere and genuine servants of the people.

Elections are important because they have real consequences for humanity. Any possible threat to the actualization of true democracy must be eliminated. We would next turn to the correct counting of ballots. Electronic voting machines have to be eliminated and replaced with paper ballots and simple marking tools. Machines of any type that are currently being used that allow any opportunity for tampering or alter the true counts of votes must be done away with.

A rock solid accounting of the votes must be established where there is no chance whatsoever for there not to be a 100% accurate count. Canada uses paper ballots that are counted by humans and they have the result at 11:00 p.m.

One who would lead and make decisions which affect the lives of millions and billions of people must know that if elected they will be performing a sacred duty. Before every debate candidates will swear an oath to speak the truth. The people must know the candidates' motivation for seeking to take on the solemn responsibility of leadership.

When a candidate shares his or her thoughts with voters they should know that they are on a witness stand and that total truth is the only option. When one has the desire to take responsibility for making wise decisions on behalf of the people there must be a deep, profound communication of the vision of that candidate. There can be no doubt in the minds of voters that they have fully understood the visions of each of the candidates.

Money should not be a factor in the selection of leaders, where their efforts on behalf of humanity are a sacred duty.

E. Find Inner Peace.

All the happiness there is in this world comes from thinking about others, and all the suffering comes from preoccupation with yourself. --Shantideva

Take a few moments and think about what you envision an ideal, New World will look like. When you are thinking about an ideal, New World please do not underestimate the amount of power that you are giving to the realization of your vision. Understand that men and women through the ages have begun revolutionary changes on planet Earth by thinking about the same things that you are thinking about at this moment.

Who are the men and women that you most admire? What are the reasons that you admire them? They were or are men and women of no more and no less worth as human beings than you. So first you must never put yourself down because there is nobody on this Earth, or who has ever lived on this Earth, who is more important or less important than another. Please know that the Creator sees all the same.

So this is New World rule number one. Never again will you treat yourself and others in any but a kind and Loving way.

How can anybody be Loving and kind to others when they are not Loving and kind to their own body, mind and soul? We know in our hearts that being Loving and kind to others is the right thing to do. Now you know that being Loving and kind to you is the right thing to do.

Hold your vision for a New World and do not doubt that your thoughts are having an effect on reality. When people have thoughts it is very interesting to observe that there is a theory that thoughts are very powerful; more powerful than we are aware of. To ponder the significance of this takes one in various, exciting directions.

An example is observed these days with the increase in communications taking place on the internet and social media like Face-book, Twitter, Skype and You-tube. This increase in communication between people is a very significant development. Before technological advances in communications people had to pay for long distance calls and that was a constraint on people to share ideas. Now there is nothing to stop folks from talking to folks all around the world.

Can we imagine the power of all the billions of thoughts shared between the people of the Earth? And then you add to that power because such a high percentage of the shared thoughts are honest and genuine. People are much freer to share their thoughts in an honest way when not talking face to face. Embarrassment constraints are absent when the person you are interacting with is hundreds or thousands of miles away.

New World rule number two. Never again will you be anything but 100% honest and genuine with yourself and with others.

Would your ideal New World vision include every man, woman and child being 100% honest and genuine at all times? Imagine how the world will look when everyone strives to be honest at all times. There would be no more misunderstandings between individuals or countries. Trust will increase to high levels and allow people to communicate all the time in a meaningful way. The content of conversations will rise to a higher level of beauty and joy.

This rising to higher levels of beauty and joy will build to higher and higher levels. Eventually there will come that point where every man, woman and child will grasp unconditional Love. This is A New World. This is Heaven on Earth.

Have you gained an awareness of the existence of the highest spiritual feeling on Earth? Have you been able to create images in your mind of literal improvements in the human condition? Would Leo Tolstoy, if he were here, come to the conclusion that real art is being created in large amounts by millions and billions of people at this moment in human history?

You the reader please understand that we are trying to articulate the highest spiritual feeling on Earth. We are trying to create a literal improvement in the human condition. That is the sole purpose of these writings. We are hoping and praying to the Creator that this work will add justice, mercy, peace and unconditional Love to this Earth at this time.

Our goal is to obliterate ego and come from humility here so that the writings are coming from the highest spiritual place possible. This work is for both you the reader and for the writer. If we can both somehow benefit here then that will be a good thing. We will have changed in a good way and then we can move on and continue exerting energy to change again in a good way. We will rise again and again and again until inevitably we are standing before unconditional Love.

We will literally arrive at the destination that is unconditional Love. At this time we will know the meaning of life. As we have risen to this understanding the points all along the way will have one common denominator. There was no turning back on our journeys to our ultimate destination. All that we learned along the way could not be unlearned. We reached a point of knowledge and continued to the next point; adding more beauteous and joyful knowledge while travelling to the next higher point

When one becomes aware of unconditional Love that man or woman finds that everything is new. This awareness makes one feel that they have reached the summit of Mt. Everest and can see for many miles in all directions. The place called unconditional Love is an otherworldly place.

New World rule number three. Never forget the place called unconditional Love.

"Thus does the miracle undo all things the world attests can never be undone". A Course in Miracles

Now that we have found Love what are we going to do with it? Let it shine. We share unconditional Love with everyone and everything. Once a man or woman finds unconditional Love it is impossible to hoard. The more you give it to others the more you receive as Love is the most powerful force in the universe and there is no end to it. It is an inexhaustible force that can never run out.

Let us pray that unconditional Love becomes known by every man, woman and child in this world. We thank the Creator for granting our wish. So be it.

We are on this Earth to evolve spiritually to attain enlightenment. Enlightenment is a state where a man or woman has come to fully understand the unconditional Love that is inside of them. Once that understanding is attained then that man or woman lives their life ruled by Love and shows the world that Love. Many believe that the time that we are living in is the time where unconditional Love is going to be experienced and understood by everyone, everywhere on Earth

Sounds like a good thing to happen. What do you think? How long is it going to be before everyone on Earth experiences and understands unconditional Love? Our intuition says this wonderful event is coming very soon. If not now, when? Today is the best day there is to start living by Love. When we recognize the fact that Love is an overwhelmingly transformative force then we will not delay. We will spread the word Love and feelings of Love at all times, everywhere we go.

Then those we interact with will accept the realization of the power of Love and live by it. You will find the rippling out of Love into the four corners of the Earth.

New World rule number four. Freely share your Love with everyone and everything.

Understand that every thought and action you ever take has consequences. Some call this the law of cause and effect. It is easy to understand if one looks at actions of a physical nature. We take an action such as reading a book (cause) and then the information in that book gives us insight and knowledge (effect). We say something stupid and hurtful to another (cause) and then we find distance and non-communication between us (effect).

We say something kind and loving to another (cause) and then we find closeness and friendship between us (effect). So the law of cause and effect is a very real law. Closely related to the law of cause and effect is good karma and bad karma. An example of creating bad karma is the previous illustration of saying something stupid and hurtful to another. An example of creating good karma is saying something kind and loving to another.

Good and bad karma is created also by our thoughts. An example of bad karma is where you think about saying something unkind and hurtful to another. Good karma is created when you think about saying kind and loving words to another. There need be no complexity involved to understand the law of cause and effect and karma. The concepts are pretty easy to understand. It is simply advisable to do good actions and think good thoughts.

Spiritual wisdom is in plentiful supply in this world. Everyone has free will to choose to live their lives however they wish. The only thing to remember is that every choice one makes has consequences. Sometimes it seems that the most profound spiritual knowledge almost seems to be too simple to be called profound. We are all in charge of our own karma, our own life, our own spiritual path and our own liberation.

New World rule number five. Reflect on the kindness of everyone you meet.

Our bodies are a marvelous mass of 50 trillion cells. We seem to have come to an under-appreciation of just how miraculous our bodies really are. We are all brothers and sisters on this Earth. The biological and genetic make-ups of all human beings are 99.99%

the same stuff. We argue and start and fight wars over the 0.01% difference comprised of the ego, greed and wrong thinking.

One could say that humanity has already completed 99.99% of the journey on the way to a New World and Heaven on Earth. We have only 0.01% of our journey to go. According to neurological studies the left hemisphere of our brains has to do with ego, language, education and all we have learned from others about the ways to operate in society or the physical realm. The right hemisphere of our brains deals with more of the spiritual matters of our lives such as intuition and perspective. This has to do with the similar terms consciousness, soul, awareness, our higher self and God/Creator.

At the core of the right hemisphere of our brains there is an accessible area of deep inner peace or what some call nirvana. All people have access to this place where one is no longer separated from Source/Creator. We are all just visitors here so what will we do during the time we are on our visit? There are two kinds of people in this life. There are those who are energy bringers and those who are energy takers. We choose at every moment which type of energy person we are going to be.

We would strive to show up 100% of the time in our interactions and take responsibility for being a bringer of energy. Realize that you can find deep inner peace at any time. Respect all people at all times and let others know that you mean them well. Value the connection to others in a way that makes you willing to try; trying is everything. Peace is a thought away and you can choose it.

New World rule number six. Value the connection to others so much that you will try.

Do not choose negative thoughts; simply say, "No, I don't want to go there." You can focus your mind on what you want to focus on. If you have had negative interactions with certain people in the past, leave it in the past and re-create a positive situation in the now. You change the game when you take responsibility and change the way you interact with others. Change your thoughts and you change your life.

Pay attention to your thoughts, tend to your own garden, own your own power and you will find that deep inner peace. We all have free and open access to that part of us that is loving, kind, joyful and magnificent. Find time to silence the chatter in your mind and develop an attitude of gratitude; become thankful for all of your blessings at all times. Cheer others on and help others.

New World rule number seven. Help others to know that inner peace is available at all times.

Find time to enter into silence.

F. Everything is Revealed.

We would guess that many of you reading these words are familiar with what is termed the near death experience (NDE). After reading a number of books and watching a number of video interviews of those who have had one or more near death experiences we must say that the subject is very fascinating.

The subject of NDE's is one that has major importance for human beings. It seems that everyone without exception is fascinated and intrigued by the phenomena. As there are no coincidences in this life one could safely say that the subject of NDE's is playing a large part in the spiritual evolution we see occurring on Earth at this time.

Given the great interest in this subject, evidenced by the number of best-selling books we see on the popular book sales lists, we can definitely say that humanity is on to something very significant.

There are a number of aspects about the stories that men and women share after having an NDE that are very intriguing.

There is a similarity between the stories shared that point to the experience being an actual, felt, real travelling to another, higher dimension of consciousness. At risk of sounding simplistic one similarity is that most (99%) considered the event real. Some have used the words "more real than Earth". Almost all (99%) of the men, women and children report experiencing a sense of overwhelming Love and peace.

Other similarities include leaving one's body and being able to see what was occurring on the hospital bed, in their homes and neighborhoods while being able to accurately describe events after returning to their bodies. Many describe being greeted, as if they were arriving at a homecoming, by the souls of relatives or friends who had passed before them. Many describe going through a tunnel towards a pinpoint of light that grows in size and intensity.

A significant similarity of the stories is that most describe the experience as indescribable. Common statements are in the vein of the following, "There are no words in the human language to describe it." So the power of the experience for these men, women and children is such that they are left in a total state of wonder and of awe. Most say that it is an experience that they will never forget as long as they live.

All who have this experience consider it a life changing event of major importance. Most, if not all, of these people have come to believe that there is no such thing as death and that there is nothing about death to fear. Most were told at a certain point in the experience that they had to return because it was "not your time" and that they had to complete some form of task back on Earth. For some that task included sharing their near death experience with others.

Many, because of the overwhelming Love and peace they were experiencing, did not want to return to their bodies. Many described how the experience felt like they were "coming home", "back home" or "home". Many describe landscapes of a type that is on Earth except much more vibrant; the colors were of a beauty and color not seen on Earth. Music is described as angelic and of such a power and beauty that no music on Earth compares.

Some have met beings who they were unfamiliar with but learned of them after coming back to Earth. An example is a man who saw and vividly remembered the face of a young girl. He had no idea who the girl was until he saw a picture of a sister who he never knew existed. This young girl died and he saw her in his NDE. He described an intense feeling of Love from the girl and her telepathically telling him that "You are Loved and cherished."

If you have not read any books on the NDE subject we would recommend doing so as the stories these men, women and children share are very inspiring and uplifting. There are many video interviews you can easily find on your computer due to the popularity of this subject. We have found a few websites, where scientists have compiled an immense amount of information and personal stories, devoted solely to the study of the near death experience.

The science has been increasing on this important subject. At this point there is a scientific consensus that those who have a near death experience have experienced a higher state of consciousness and that the events are real. At the beginning there were those who attributed the experience to oxygen deprivation of the brain and such. Any scientist today who sees the experience as anything but real may be considered as someone who believes the Earth is flat.

Once again we would suggest that you find some of the stories these folks are sharing. You can rest assured that you will be glad that you did.

Of all the fantastic aspects of the NDE subject this writer finds the "life review" to be most fascinating, and perhaps most important, aspect for study by humanity.

We desire to delve into the discussion of the life review in such a way that the overwhelming importance of the subject is conveyed to you and the many others. As writers have been described as wordsmiths we are very concerned that we bring this information to you in a way that is revelatory and conveys the immense spiritual power of the message.

Up to this point in this writing we have gone along fairly steadily. Now we will be totally honest with you. This writer has come to the life review process described by these people and we have felt a palpable warning to take great care when writing on this subject. We have an increased awareness that those who read these words will be influenced, and that they must be influenced in a good way.

We would say that this writer has not experienced a life review and suggests very strongly to you the reader to find the accounts and descriptions of those who have.

We would ask of you the reader that you please forgive the writer if he fails to match the message of the life review with the highest level of spiritual communication required.

Please know that we consider the ideas and concepts surrounding the life review described by those who have had a near death experience absolutely important. We pray to the Creator that we can write the following in a good way that conveys the sacred.

For the life review is a sacred spiritual experience.

Those reading these words that have had a near death experience and a life review will forgive the writer for any inaccuracy. For one to attempt to describe an experience of overwhelming profundity and power is probably taking on a more difficult task than climbing Mt. Everest. To start, when we first heard the stories of those who had the life review we were stunned and overwhelmed.

The life review is described as almost like watching the movie of your entire life. As opposed to what we consider a movie of two hours which can only show glimpses of the story, the life review contains every action and thought of our lives. Somehow an entire lifetime is reviewed in an accelerated way which does not omit any action or thought, no matter how insignificant.

We see absolutely every action. We see absolutely every thought. We are told in the spiritual texts that nothing is hidden. With the life review we find confirmation of the truth that indeed nothing is hidden. The most dazzling revelation of those who experienced the life review was their description of feelings when interacting with others.

At every point of their life reviews the man or woman felt what those they were interacting with felt. For example say a boy was eight years old and struck one of his friends. He then felt his friend's physical and mental pain. Perhaps then a short time later he apologizes to his friend for striking him. At that point he would feel his friend's relief and gladness that they were now able to be friends again.

He not only feels the other boy's physical and mental pain, but he feels what everyone who experiences consequences felt, from the initial event of hitting his friend. The boy who was hit goes home and finds his mother asking him what happened. Now the man having the life review will feel what the mother of the struck boy feels, because he was hit by his friend. He will feel the mother's emotions and the need to protect and soothe her son.

The man having the life review will see the thoughts of everyone affected as a consequence of his action of hitting his friend. Perhaps at this point the mother of the struck boy goes to his mother to try and resolve the matter. Now he will see the thoughts, and feel the feelings of every consequential participant. He feels his own mother's concern when she has to determine the proper course for handling this problem with him.

Then his mother talks to his father about the matter. He feels what his father is feeling when his father hears about the incident. Perhaps his father becomes upset and yells at the son's younger sister who is playing the piano and she starts to cry. Now he feels the hurt of his little sister. These revelations continue to that point where the consequences of his action of hitting his friend end.

Consider that your every action is recorded in the book of life. Some use the term Akashic records or Hall of Records. Consider that your every thought is recorded. Consider that every consequence of your every action is recorded. Consider that every consequence of your every thought is recorded.

When the person having the life review comes to those points where they have done or thought something of a negative nature, they feel the other person's pain and suffer deep regret. Some have expressed feeling unworthy and the feeling of being a spiritual failure. Can we imagine having such an experience? We are reminded of those actions and thoughts which caused us regret.

Positive actions and thoughts are also experienced. When one takes a positive action such as saying or doing something kind and Loving for another we feel the joy and Love of the other. We see the consequence of our action when the person we helped goes on to help another in the same manner. We then feel the good feelings of the person who was helped by the person we helped.

Perhaps the person who was helped by the person we helped goes home and hugs his dog then goes to the garden and lovingly takes care of his plants. We feel the joy created in the animal as well as the joy of the plants, all as a result of our initial good deed.

The life review is so overwhelmingly profound that one is left with nothing but complete awe for the Creator.

The examples we used were simple illustrations of descriptions by those who have had the near death experience and the life review. We have learned that nothing is hidden. Absolutely everything is revealed.

The actions we used to describe the life review thus far are at one end of the spectrum of human actions. With these examples there are relatively few consequences. At the other end of the spectrum there are actions and thoughts which have the most tremendous consequences for humanity and the Creation.

Let us imagine what a life review experienced by some historical figures would look like.

Let us imagine Adolf Hitler's life review experience. This will be very difficult as one cannot fathom the darkness of the feelings this soul must have experienced.

We could imagine that Hitler had experienced some positivity in his childhood. Of course there was the point where his thoughts and subsequent actions turned in a more negative direction. It is vexing to consider that soul who was Adolf Hitler. Can we imagine the crushing weight of regret, remorse and angst upon feeling what those many people felt as a result of his actions and thoughts? And then that soul had to feel the even heavier weight of all of the consequences of pain and suffering.

Due to the choices by Adolf Hitler to descend into negative actions and thoughts of an unimaginable darkness, that soul suffered negative consequences in equal magnitude.

One would think that soul, while experiencing what he was responsible for, had to have been sobbing to such painful depths, and feeling such overwhelming grief that it was unimaginable. One could sense that the experience was similar to what one feels when one loses a Loved one, of an intensity a million times stronger. See in your mind's eye the soul of Adolf Hitler experiencing the pain at the death of one for which he was responsible, followed by another, and another, and another...

There have been many who have lived on this Earth whose souls must have gone through the same unbelievable fire of guilt, remorse and regret. This could be the fire described in the spiritual texts.

His disciples asked him, and said unto him: "Wilt thou that we fast? And how shall we pray? Shall we give alms? And what rules shall we observe in eating?" Jesus said: "Do not lie; and that which you hate, do not do. For all things are revealed before

Heaven. For there is nothing hidden which will not be made manifest, and there is nothing covered which shall remain without being uncovered." –The Gospel of Thomas

At the other end of the spectrum of historical figures, how could the life review experienced by Mother Teresa be imagined?

As Mother Teresa was venerated and adored by many millions, we can imagine a positivity of Love with her soul's life review.

We can see in our mind's eye the positive feelings that Mother Teresa gave during her life, coming back to her at many points, from those she expressed Love to. We can see the amount of Love that was spread on this planet Earth through the beautiful trail of consequences of her actions and thoughts. We can feel her joy as she feels how others felt at the times of their interactions; with those she helped and those she sacrificed for.

One can come to the conclusion that the soul called Mother Teresa had no moments of guilt, remorse or regret as she experienced her life review. The soul known as Mother Teresa made the choice of Love and service to her fellow humanity, when at the point of decision. Mother Teresa understood the choice was Love or keeping Love hidden.

As she chose all during her life to serve humanity while spreading joy and Love, her life review confirmed the absolute power of Love to make a positive difference in the physical realm on the Earth. Mother Teresa was faced with the same choices that all human beings are faced with. She chose Love and service to humanity.

The life review as described by those men and women who have had the near death experience gives humanity proof positive of the truth contained in many spiritual writings. We learn that the spiritual realm is an actual place and that we reap what we have sown. We are reminded that there is a judgment day.

What those who have the life review say is that we are not judged by anyone orentity, but that we judge ourselves. Some have described being accompanied by an angel or other being with a Loving presence. The review is like a movie from the moment we are born to the moment we die. We come to realize that we could have made better choices.

During the life review we understand that our life could have been much more joyful and Loving. Then we are able to see the life we could have lived if we had made better choices. There are feelings of regret for those choices which we made that were unwise and we want to go back and do it right.

We learn that the true nature of everything is Love. We are astonished and wish we had known this all along. Those times where we feel the pain of those we hurt are the true definition of hell. The experience is a moment of truth that teaches with Love and compassion. There is no judgment from God but, as we mentioned, we judge our own just completed lives.

We are here on Earth to learn how to grow our souls. The life review brings the realization of something you were not aware of. Unseen and unknown truths are revealed in the life review. We find that we have missed the mark and it is painful to realize that we have gone wrong. Anything that does not align with Love causes us pain and that pain is the distance between us and God.

Many look on the experience of reviewing their lives as a supreme gift. They come back to God. Many have learned acceptance as well. After coming back to Earth the acceptance of others' views, purposes and life paths became a way of life. Tolerance of others became important as well. Most become much more altruistic and unselfishly concerned about the welfare of others.

The vast majority of those who have had the near death experience now have no fear of death because they have learned that there is no such thing as death.

The responsibility is placed at the feet of each individual soul to make their choices along the journey.

As we have learned a little about the life review we are left with a strong sense of wonder. When one considers the mind of the Creator or God or Allah one is left speechless. Words cannot describe the emotions that this subject produces.

It seems that there is a very strong interest in these types of experiences. There is a tremendous amount to be learned from becoming aware of what these men, women and children are saying.

We believe that the ideas, emotions, feelings and honesty contained in these folks' personal accounts have the potential to greatly influence the world and the spiritual evolution of humanity.

G. The Highest Love.

Greater Love hath no man than this, that one lay down his life for his friends. —Jesus Christ

We hope that thus far into these writings that you have been helped and gained insight regarding the power of Love. We have tried to convey ideas and concepts that will improve the lives of all who read these words. One of the folks who had the near death experience said that there were no coincidences in this life.

We sometimes do not give a second thought to the various experiences we all have in our lives. We go into situations and do not consider that there are options as far as what actions and decisions we take during every moment. It would seem that this is very important to know so that we think before we act.

Let us use the example of a rude sales clerk. After reading about the life review will you now show much more patience and try to leave that sales clerk with kindness and good thoughts? Or will you become upset and say unkind words which only magnify the negativity of the situation? It is always our choice in every situation what and how to contribute.

In your relationships with your family and friends do you now have another perspective as to how you can take control and responsibility for your actions? We hope that all who have read these words have become more aware of the magnificence of this life and will shed the petty and unimportant. We would seem to be better off if we would make it a habit of looking at the big picture.

What do we mean when we say the big picture? The big picture is the realization that the true nature of everything is Love. We have a great appreciation for being able to share some thoughts with others with these writings. One of our goals as we mentioned at the beginning was to communicate the highest spiritual feeling on the Earth. This is a tall order.

All we can say about this is that we have tried to give you all that we thought was important to share. We believe that you are sure that we have been sincere. Believe it or not we would like everyone who reads these words to experience in a real way the highest possible feeling of a spiritual nature available to human beings. We would wish that you the reader experience the highest Love.

Our vision is for the human race to come to the realization that unconditional Love is the answer to every problem we as humanity faces. We know that many have tried to convey the same message through the ages. We are attempting to, perhaps, come to the issue of communicating the powerful message of unconditional Love in a different way that makes a real, positive difference. Maybe just being totally honest and saying what is on one's mind about Love is all that will be required.

When one has this type of vision, that of seeing the enlightenment of every man, woman and child on Earth, one is aware of the immensity of actualizing that vision. Perhaps, as we have learned in the life review, there is power in our thoughts that is available to accomplish humanity's complete enlightenment. Could it be that if enough people thought about enlightenment for humanity and A New World/Heaven on Earth being created that it will make the difference? We believe that this is possible.

Understand that the writer has thought about using words in a way that there will be a literal improvement in the human condition. This was what Leo Tolstoy thought real art is, if you remember our mention of this at various points of these writings. Perhaps we could say that this work is real art, according to Tolstoy, if just one reader was somehow helped or their life may have been improved as a result of reading these words.

The writer of these words is thinking about how to communicate so as to improve the conditions for every person, all life and all things on this Earth. We thought that maybe doing a possible life review for those who are responsible for GMO foods and crops, those who are in the financial system who are responsible for fraudulent actions and those who have power to change the global climate change situation would be useful.

Perhaps a life review of someone who is responsible for causing wars and the deaths of innocent women and children could be written. Or someone who has information important for humanity but is constrained because they could lose their journalism position at a major media corporation.

Maybe those people are having lessons learned that are important for their evolution. One feels torn between whether to name names and blowing the whistle and trying to come at the historical problems on Earth from the highest possible spiritual plane possible. In order to actualize the vision of A New World/Heaven on Earth one has to fight not to give up.

Surely you the reader have had the thought while reading these words that this writer is out there. Albert Einstein said that imagination is more important than knowledge. That statement by Einstein is surely true in the case of attempting to enlighten all of humanity. One remembers the song "Imagine" by the late John Lennon.

Imagine there's no heaven, it's easy if you try

No hell below us, above us only sky

Imagine all the people, living for today

Imagine there's no countries, it isn't hard to do

Nothing to kill and die for, and no religion too

Imagine all the people, living life in peace

You may say I'm a dreamer, but I'm not the only one

I hope someday you'll join us, and the world will be as one

Imagine no possessions, I wonder if you can

No need for greed or hunger, a brotherhood of man

Imagine all the people, sharing all the world

You may say I'm a dreamer, but I'm not the only one

I hope someday you'll join us, and the world will live as one.

You would have to agree that John Lennon was a true artist. This song "Imagine" is one of the greatest examples of musical art we will ever come across. Even though the song seems rather simple the message is expressing very profound wisdom. It would have been interesting to have seen John Lennon grow to old age. Can we imagine the works of art he would have continued to create?

Another artist who was admired for his efforts to bring humanity together was Bob Marley. Let's look at the lyrics to "One Love".

One Love, one heart, let's get together and feel alright

Hear the children crying, hear the children crying

Saying: "Give thanks and praise to the Lord and I will feel alright

Saying let's get together and feel alright

Let them all pass all their dirty remarks

There is one question I'd really like to ask

Is there peace for the hopeless sinner, who has hurt all mankind just to save his beliefs?

One Love, one heart, what about? Let's get together and feel alright

As it was in the beginning, so shall it be in the end

Give thanks and praise to the Lord and I will feel alright

Let's get together and feel alright

Let's get together to fight this holy Armageddon

So when the man comes there will be no, no doom

Have pity on those whose chances grow thinner

There ain't no hiding place from the Father of Creation

I'm pleading to mankind oh, Lord!

Give thanks and praise to the Lord and I will feel alright.

John Lennon and Bob Marley are no longer with us. We can say that they are still with us in that we are still moved by their artistic creations. We wonder what we will leave to future generations. There are but a handful of people who have come to be as well known as John Lennon or Bob Marley. We can say that for these two artists that fame and fortune were not at the top of their list of goals.

One could surmise that these artists wanted to achieve goals that were in line with creating a better world. Did John Lennon and Bob Marley succeed? We would say that, yes, they did succeed. Both artists conveyed the highest spiritual feeling and those who were profoundly moved by their messages were improved as a result.

It is sometimes difficult to speak about truth and spirituality. One has to wonder what the true cause of this reluctance is. It may be that there comes a point when discussing truth and spirituality where there is a collision with the great mystery. This is that point where the discussion can no longer reveal anything because nobody but the truly enlightened has a certain, direct knowledge.

Perhaps folks have a hard time colliding with mystery because it is evidence that we don't know. This may explain the turning away from sharing thoughts on spiritual matters. We have some excellent examples of truths from those who have had the near death experience. For this writer reading personal accounts and viewing videos on the near death experience have been very inspiring and resonate as truth.

There are a few passages we would share with you here. These come from a book that was found in Nag Hammadi, Egypt in 1945 along with thirteen other books now known collectively as The Gnostic Library. The book from the library that the following passages comes from is The Secret Book of John.

Six Questions About the Soul.

I asked the savior (Jesus Christ), "Lord, will every soul be saved and enter the pure light?"

He replied, "You are asking an important question, one it will be impossible to answer for anyone who is not a member of the unmoved race. They are the people upon whom the spirit of life will descend and the power will enable them to be saved and to become perfect and worthy of greatness. They expunge evil from themselves and they will care nothing for wickedness, wanting only that which is not corrupt. They will achieve freedom from rage, envy, jealousy, desire or craving."

"The physical body will negatively affect them. They wear it as they look forward to the time when they will meet up with those who will remove it. Those people deserve indestructible eternal life. They endure everything, bearing up under everything that happens so that they can deserve the good and inherit life eternal."

Then I asked him, "Lord, what about the souls who did not do these things even though the spirit of life's power descended on them?"

He answered, "If the spirit descends to people they will be transformed and saved. The power descends on everyone and without it, no one can even stand up. After they are born, if the spirit of life increases in them, power comes to them and their souls are strengthened. Nothing then can lead them astray into wickedness. But if the artificial spirit comes into people, it leads them astray."

Then I said, "Lord, when souls come out of the flesh where do they go?"

He replied, smiling, "If the soul is strong it has more of power than it has of the artificial spirit and so it flees from wickedness. With the assistance of the incorruptible one that soul is saved and attains eternal rest."

I then asked him, "Lord, what of the souls of the people who do not know whose people they are? Where do they go?"

He responded, "In those people the artificial spirit has grown strong and they have gone astray. Their souls are burdened, drawn to wickedness, and cast into forgetfulness. When they come forth from the body, such a soul is given over to the powers created by the rulers, bound in chains, and cast into prison again. Around and around it goes until it manages to become free from forgetfulness through knowledge. And so, eventually, it becomes perfect and is saved."

Then I asked, "Lord, how does the soul shrink down so as to be able to enter its mother or a man?"

He was happy to be asked this and said, "You are truly blessed because you have understood. The soul should be guided by another within whom is the spirit of life. It will be saved by that means and accordingly will not have to enter the body again."

And I said, "Lord, what happens to the souls of people who achieved true knowledge, but who turned away from it?"

He said to me, "Demons of property will take them to a place where there is no possibility of repentance. There they will stay until the time when those who blasphemed against the spirit will be tortured and subjected to punishment forever."

If you would be interested in studying Gnostic texts/writings www.gnosis.org has a large library that you can read.

This excerpt from The Secret Book of John is very revealing. There seems to be a reference to reincarnation where Jesus speaks about "...such a soul is given over to the powers created by the rulers, bound in chains, and cast into prison again. Around and around it goes until it manages to become free from forgetfulness through knowledge. And so, eventually, it becomes perfect and is saved."

Reincarnation is a touchy subject as many religions have the belief that there is one life to be lived, and that reincarnation is erroneous. Other spiritual traditions hold the belief in reincarnation, most notably Buddhism. One would read the previous paragraph and can come to no other conclusion but that Jesus is talking about reincarnation.

Some hold that we (as souls) have had many hundreds of previous lives. We have been and done it all; we have been rich, poor, male, female, good, bad and ugly. This writer would lean toward the reality of reincarnation as it explains the unbelievable lives of many on this planet. We are speaking about those who endure immense suffering.

As an example there is a theory that a soul will decide to come into their next incarnation and be a young child who dies at a very young age. That soul decided that the lessons learned by others from the experience made it an important sacrifice to make. When one considers that we are souls in a body and not bodies with a soul we come to understand that we are forever beings. Our soul is our essence and never dies.

We lean toward the reality of living many lives. But whether reincarnation is the truth of our reality or we get one life it still is an unbelievable experience. If reincarnation is the truth then we strive to get on the good path and off the wheel of life, death and rebirth. If we get only one life then we try to get on the good path to achieve a heavenly realm.

Personally we cannot figure out how a loving Creator/God could send a soul to eternal damnation. It may be that, as stated previously, hell is the part of the life review where we feel the pain we have caused others. We have all felt regret for saying or doing something which hurts another. There can be no doubt that this regret is a hellish experience.

It would seem that all of the spiritual traditions have an amount of truth in their philosophies and writings. One could say that all of the various spiritual traditions are but individual facets of the same diamond. That diamond is absolute truth.

So where do we go now? We try to be good and get on the right road.

What can we say about the "artificial spirit"? This term was used in the excerpt from The Secret Book of John. Our best guess is that the artificial spirit represents all that one must overcome to attain enlightenment. These are rage, envy, jealousy, desire and craving. Elements of our lower nature must be defeated before knowledge and wisdom can be attained.

Perhaps many of you are aware of the term bodhisattva. For those readers who are not, a bodhisattva is an enlightened being who forgoes or postpones nirvana until all beings have attained enlightenment. Out of compassion the bodhisattva waits for nirvana and enters another incarnation until all can come with them by becoming enlightened. We believe that there are many bodhisattvas on Earth right now as evidenced by the spiritual evolution being experienced by humanity.

It is truly amazing to think about these things. One considers the exquisite state of the life process and is left with a feeling of awe that is indescribable.

Consider the words of Jesus here and tell me you are not just absolutely blown away.

"Even the least among you can do all that I have done, and greater things."

This is a statement by Jesus which needs to be thought about deeply. Let us try to determine what some possible greater things could be. Could the coming together of humanity in unconditional Love and the creation of A New Earth/Heaven on Earth be greater?

Do you think if we asked Jesus if he thought that humanity's creation of A New Earth/Heaven on Earth was one of the greater things he was talking about, that he would answer yes or no?

With the absolute power of unconditional Love everything is possible.

This includes the creation of A New World. A Heaven on Earth.

And now we say "Amen": for Christ has come to dwell in the abode you set for him before time was, in calm eternity. The journey closes, ending at the place where it began. No trace of it remains. Not one illusion is accorded faith, and not one spot of darkness remains to hide the face of Christ from anyone. –A Course in Miracles

H. Living Love.

Can we imagine how many men, women and children on this planet Earth are, right now, holding a vision of A New World? We would estimate that these folks number in the millions, perhaps billions. When we simply understand that there are a tremendous number of human beings who have thought about the same things covered in these writings we understand why we are witnessing significant spiritual evolution on Earth.

You and I are living in an extremely powerful period. This period of human history that we are experiencing is one that will go down as the time that humanity got it right. In a sense we could say that there has been the discovery of a new branch of science. We can call this new branch of science spiritual engineering. The new science has to do with consciousness and the raising of consciousness.

The prerequisite to entering the study and practice of spiritual engineering is unconditional Love. Once a person gains an awareness of unconditional Love then that person is ready to help build A New World, where everyone understands unconditional Love. Just as in all of the other scientific fields, the discoveries which opened that field to study were a major advancement for humanity. Consider the discovery of electricity, the internal combustion engine, the printing press and the first computers.

All of the discoveries through history have contributed to the physical reality we are now witnessing and experiencing. We would not see jets in the sky if the Wright brothers had not led the way. We would not have all of the wonderful tools for communicating around the world if there were not those who spent the time and made the effort to create. The first computer was called ENIAC and was so large that it filled an entire room.

Now we have much more computing ability than was contained in ENIAC available to us that will fit in the palm of our hands. As a result of men and women spending tremendous amounts of energy in the study of the various engineering fields there have been vast amounts of information compiled. The same can be said about all of the various fields of study.

Everyone is familiar with the number of fields of study available from schools of all levels. Each field of study is comprised of a curriculum or group of related courses. The student takes the courses, learns the field and enters the world to practice what he or she has learned. Some fields of study have a greater impact on humanity than others. Given our perception of the most important issues facing humanity the genetic engineers, the finance majors and the climate scientists are in fields that are very important at this time.

Genetic engineers are aware of the facts surrounding genetically modified organisms and the negative consequences of allowing these creations into the Earth's environment. Finance majors are aware of the operations of the monetary system and what is required to solve worldwide problems of an economic nature. Climate scientists and environmental engineers have read all of the science surrounding global climate change and have solutions for this Earth threatening phenomena.

Those who studied broadcasting and journalism were learning very soon after graduating from university that the ideal they held about bringing the news in a truthful way to the people was an ideal which held some risk. Many quickly learned in reality what a "killed story" was all about. Many who entered managerial positions at broadcasting and media organizations learned quickly not to be the nail that stands out amongst many nails. The nail that stands out is the one that gets hammered.

Fortunately there are alternative media where one can find the truth about Earth realities. The ability of human beings to communicate freely has been the impetus for humanity to move strongly against current societal problems in a large way. We see evidence of this with the mass movements of people in various countries around the world which are trying to create better situations for themselves and others.

Due to the massive amount of truth being shared by human beings all around Earth the human collective has gained a tremendous amount of previously withheld knowledge. This great increase in knowledge of Earth realities has impelled people to take action.

Perhaps a genetic scientist who works at a corporation to make a living finds a place to go on his or her computer where he or she can let others know what the dangers are. Perhaps a man or woman is in the belly of the beast in a Wall Street firm and finds his or her outlet on the computer, where they can let others know the real truth and solutions. Perhaps the climate scientist finds his or her outlet on the computer where they can clear their conscience while waiting for the good changes.

Can we imagine the profound amount of truth that is being communicated on the internet? Blog sites, chat rooms, groups of like minded people, people typing in their thoughts with remarks and all of the social media add up to a huge amount of truthful information being shared. This is good for humanity. One can imagine that many of the people who chose to participate in this exchange of ideas are feeling an immense sense of freedom.

In essence the technology allowing this free sharing of thoughts, ideas and truth is a freedom superhighway with billions of lanes. Whereas in the past folks were constrained in the sharing of ideas because there were so few freedom lanes, today finds humanity in possession of the greatest, freedom producing gift the Creator has ever granted.

One can see comparisons between the life review, Akashic records or Hall of Records and the mind boggling amount of information, now available to humanity at their fingertips and the keyboard.

We see in our mind's eye the billions of good thoughts that are being shared by humanity. We imagine the billions of words that are being used to express those good thoughts. We do a search of those billions of words for the words Love, unconditional Love and Infinite Love. Our search result shows us that unconditional Love is being shared by humanity.

Thy will is done, complete and perfectly, and all Creation recognizes you and knows you as the only source it has. Clear in your likeness does the light shine forth from everything that lives and moves in you. For we have reached where all of us are one, and we are home where you would have us be. –A Course in Miracles

I. A New World.

It is interesting to think about time. Let us look at the similarities between the amount of time that is called a day and the amount of time that is called a year.

A day begins with the sun rising in the east. What was darkness now, bit by bit, becomes brighter as the sun moves upward. As the sun moves directly over us we see the world brightly. Then the sun moves in its usual way to the west. As it moves in its natural way to the west the amount of light decreases, bit by bit, until sunset and the darkness of night.

All living things arise at daybreak, go through the day bit by bit, and enjoy the noonday sun. As the sun moves to the west, it sets. All living things lie down during the darkness of night.

A year begins in the spring when new life begins. The summer sees rapid growth of all living things. Fall finds the ripening with gratitude and joy for the abundance. Winter sees all things lie down for sleep.

All living things enjoy the new life of spring. All grow during the summer. All partake of the fall harvest and give thanks to the Creator. Winter is the time of introspection for all living things.

All living things are born on this Earth. All grow rapidly during childhood. All living things enjoy the summer of their lives. All come to maturity and the harvest of knowledge and wisdom. All give thanks to the Creator. All enter the winter of their lives and lie down to sleep.

This is the circle of life that never ends.

Thank you for reading these words.

####

www.ingramcontent.com/pod-product-compliance
Lightning Source LLC
Chambersburg PA
CBHW070551290526
45790CB00002B/634